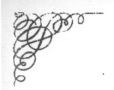

To

_____

From

_____

Gifts of the Wise Men

Gifts of the Wise Men

A Treasury of Christmas Stories

COLLEEN REECE

Kregel
Publications

Gifts of the Wise Men

© 2004 by Colleen Reece

ISBN 0-8254-3607-9

Cover & Interior Design: John M. Lucas

Introduction

inter and Christmas. Familyness. Warm, spiced apple cider. Cozy evenings and good books. Best of all, the celebration of Jesus' birth, God's gift to us of His only Son.

A kaleidoscope of Christmas memories come from my childhood years spent living near Darrington, a small, western Washington logging town. There I learned to read beneath the rays of a kerosene lamp, and we made paper chains for the tree Dad marked in the nearby forest long before snow hid possible flaws. Each year, the perfect tree touched our ten-foot dining room ceiling in what was once a one-room school where Mom taught all eight grades.

We stretched hard-earned money to provide gifts for numerous relatives. We saved and ironed paper and ribbon from year to year. Tree ornaments made from the tops of fruit and vegetable cans reflected flames from candles on the buffet. A treetop angel silently announced the Good News of Jesus' birth. Anticipation mounted while we learned parts for school and church-school programs that in those days faithfully included the story of the Nativity.

Precious and valuable. Fragrant and pleasing. Some bittersweet, all lasting. Yet certain Christmases stand out. My first "store-bought" holiday. The first Christmas after electricity came to our side of the river and we could have colored lights. The first "missing person" Christmas, with my older brother overseas. A few without snow. Sad Christmases without Dad. Then Mom.

The Wise Men brought their best gifts. We were taught to do the same, no matter how simple that "best" was. It shaped our "holy-days"—and still does.

The following story reminds us what the best gifts truly are.

The Christmas List

A certain man dreamed he saw Jesus writing in a book and surrounded by angels. "What is Jesus doing?" the man whispered to an angel who stood nearby.

"He is making a wish list," the angel quietly answered.

Jesus making a wish list? No one ever heard of such a thing, the astonished man thought to himself.

Jesus went on writing.

A great longing to know what was in the book possessed the dreamer. His heart pounded. What if there were something on Jesus' list that he could give? His excitement vanished. He had no gold, no frankincense, no myrrh; nothing valuable enough to present to the Holy One. Sadness swept through him like a mighty river in full flood.

Jesus stopped writing, smiled, and beckoned the man to come near.

Trembling with awe, the dreamer stumbled forward until he stood at the Master's side.

Jesus looked deep into the man's eyes, then asked, "Why do you grieve?"

"I have nothing to give You," the man brokenly replied.

Jesus shook His head and handed the dreamer His book. "Not so. You have that which I want above all else. Read for yourself."

The man stared at the clean, white page with its single entry. Not gold. Not frankincense. Not myrrh. Just the words, *All I want is the hearts of those I came to save.*

The man awakened. He leaped from bed, fell to his knees, and cried, "Lord, my heart is Yours. I will also try to bring others to You."

The shouts of angels rejoicing echoed deep in the dreamer's soul.

And an image of the Master's smile engraved itself on a surrendered human heart.

PART 1
Gold

But where can wisdom be found? Where does understanding dwell? . . .
It cannot be bought with the finest gold.
—Job 28:12,15

"Store-Bought" Christmas

My nine-year-old right hand curled inside my shabby mitten until it ached. My heart pounded. Even the tall buildings I usually gaped at on our rare visits to the city fifty miles from the tiny Washington State logging town where I'd been born had lost their charm. All my attention focused on three five-and-dime stores in the same block. World War II and gas rationing had ended. For the first time in years, our family could go on a real Christmas shopping trip instead of having to make do with mail orders.

My sweaty fingers clutched a vast fortune—four shining, silver quarters—the means to purchase gifts for Mom, Dad, and my two brothers. It had taken weeks of washing windows and scrubbing cupboards to save a whole dollar's worth of pennies, nickels, and dimes. Thoughts of how wonderful it would be to give "store-bought" instead of homemade gifts danced in my head like the visions of sugar plums in *The Night Before Christmas*. They also removed any temptation to spend the money on myself.

We finally reached Everett. Dad and Mom turned me loose while they shopped, a perfectly safe thing to do in those days. I wandered up and down the aisles between counters of gifts that dazzled eyes unaccustomed to such splendor. Mom's gift proved easy, an artificial Christmas corsage—the first I'd seen. Holly. Ribbon. Even a tiny cone sprinkled with glitter to resemble snow. I held my breath, looked at the price and inwardly cheered. Four quarters divided by four gifts meant twenty-five cents each, the exact price of the corsage.

Next came my older brother's present. I don't remember what it was, but it also cost a quarter. Pride filled me. I'd been through each of the stores just once, yet after only two hours, half my shopping was done!

Then I hit a snag. On a nearby counter a wonderful monkey bank grinned at me. My little brother would love it. Friendly painted grin, blue pants, red jacket; the monkey tipped his hat when the clerk obligingly dropped in a penny. I had to have it for Randy. I held my breath and looked at the tag. Oh, no! Twenty-nine cents.

I backed away, my joy in ruins at the monkey's painted boots. I can't remember a more bitter childhood disappointment. I never once thought of finding my folks and asking for four pennies. They didn't have much money, and we'd been raised to not ask for things. I went to the other stores. Nothing appealed to me. Why did I have to see the charming bank when I couldn't buy it for my brother?

Who is to say childish disappointments are not recognized by the Author of Christmas? I don't call it a miracle, but it was more than chance that through my misery I spied a display of bandannas like Dad used for handkerchiefs in his woods work. The sign read: 21 cents.

"May I help you?" the clerk asked.

"A navy blue bandanna, please," I quavered, holding out a quarter. She put the change into my hand and gave me the bandanna. I rushed from the store and ran as fast as I could, pursued by the fear the bank had been sold. It hadn't. The same painted monkey face smiled at me while I counted out the last of my silver hoard— and four dull pennies.

My family loved the gifts. Relatives obligingly gave Randy a few coins. He gleefully laughed each time the monkey tipped his hat. I can't remember what I received, just the joy in my family's faces.

Two thousand years ago Wise Men brought their best gifts to Bethlehem. On my first "store-bought" Christmas I understood how they felt. I still do.

Amaris and the Prophecy: A Story from Long Ago

*A*maris, whose name meant "whom God hath promised," feverishly worked to complete the promised garment before the dying sun's rays disappeared behind the rooftops of surrounding buildings. The muffled cries of a city freeing itself from daily tasks in anticipation of the coming holy days echoed outside her small shop. Inside, half-completed garments lay carelessly tossed aside by the most sought-after worker in the dusty Street of the Weavers.

"Mother?" Twelve-year-old Petra's soft voice interrupted the silence that had fallen while crowds thinned and hurried home before dusk. "Will you be finished soon?"

"Yes, my child." The workworn fingers flew faster than ever. "Light the candle, child."

Petra obeyed. "I will be glad when you finish that plain brown garment." She fingered a shimmering heap of silk. "Why did you not do the blue tunic first?"

Amaris shook her head. "Your mother is a foolish woman. When a man begged me to make a warm garment for his master, I could not refuse. It is finished, but the tunic is not." She held up a flawless robe and laid it aside.

Her daughter smiled. "You would have finished the tunic, as well, if the poor dog with a broken leg had not taken you from your work." She nodded toward a straw-filled wooden box in the corner. "You always help those who need you, don't you, Mother?"

"Too often!" Amaris snatched up the blue silk, straining to see where she had left off. "If only Lady Veronica waits until the morrow to send her servants for this."

Alas for the weaver's hopes. Even as she spoke, a knock thundered on the door. A young man with the pierced earlobe of a slave haughtily strode into the room. He stared at the shining garment Amaris held. "Woman, why is Lady Veronica's tunic not finished?"

"Please come back when the cock crows," Amaris told him.

"No." The arrogant slave's eyes glittered. "You can expect no more work from my lady."

"Wait," Amaris pleaded. "I myself will bring the tunic to the guard who stands at the gate."

"Do not trouble yourself." He stormed out to the sound of the injured dog's howling.

A tear escaped. Amaris thrust the tunic away so it would not be spotted. "This is what comes of having a tender heart," she told Petra. She sighed. "Now the prophecy cannot come true."

"Prophecy?" Petra's eyes sparkled in the candlelight. "Tell me, Mother."

A faraway look crept into Amaris's tired eyes. "When I was your age, an old woman my parents said was a prophetess put her hands on my head. She said I would have three opportunities for greatness in my life. She warned me to choose wisely and recognize them when they came. I still remember the feeling of wonder. I? Great? It seemed impossible."

"You are already the greatest among the weavers," Petra loyally protested. "Why did you never tell me about the prophecy?"

"It happened so long ago. Times were hard. Father was falsely imprisoned and died. Mother followed soon after. A few years later, I met a kind weaver. Ezra was older than I, but loving. He taught me all his weaving secrets. Both Jews and Romans sought us out. When you came after many years had passed, we knew great joy and thanked God. Yet even before your father died, I had lost my first opportunity for greatness." Her lips twisted bitterly.

Round-eyed, Petra could only stare.

"We had a large royal order, but I could not withstand the appeal of a young man who needed soft cloth for a child. I gave him the best we had . . . although it meant that I did not have enough cloth for the royal order."

"Was Father angry?"

"No. He said he was glad for my kind heart." Tears of remembrance gushed.

"As am I, Mother." A small hand patted Amaris's fingers.

"I determined never to do such a thing again. I kept my promise until three years ago, when I had a second opportunity for greatness by making royal apparel for the palace. But a fisherman pleaded with me to make sails for his boat. I told him I was no maker of tents, but somehow I could not send him away." She laid aside the blue silk. "Now my last opportunity is gone."

Petra's eyes overflowed. "Yet is it not great to help poor people?"

"Of course, my child." Amaris sighed again over the lost prophecy. "Come, we must sleep."

The holy days passed quietly. Amaris and Petra stayed off the noisy, bustling streets except for a brief visit to the Temple. Never too familiar with the other weavers, they did not hear the news of the city until many days had passed. Then an excited neighbor told them, "The veil of the Temple is rent in twain."

Amaris' heart lurched. "It is not possible!" A thought brought hope. If true, a new veil would be needed. What if she were given a final chance to undo her foolish choices?

No summons came. One night Amaris crept to her pallet, bone-weary and defeated. She awakened from a troubled sleep. Petra stood beside her bed.

Moonlight bathed the girl with radiance. "Mother," she whispered. "The prophecy is fulfilled."

"What?" Amaris struggled to understand.

Petra flung herself into her mother's arms. "You chose right every time."

"No!" Amaris cried. "Three times I had the opportunity. Three times I failed."

Petra's hold tightened. "Oh, no, Mother. The figure said so."

"Figure?" Had Petra gone mad?

"In glistening white. I do not know if it was real or a dream." Petra's eyes widened. "The figure said, 'Your mother has chosen greatness without knowing it. The cloth she gave to a young man long ago became swaddling clothes for Jesus, the Son of God, born in a manger.

"'The heavy cloth that bruised her fingers became sails on a fisherman's boat. From that boat, the Promised One offered hope to the world.

"'The brown garment, woven without seam, was won by the casting of lots when Jesus no longer had use for it. Tell Amaris the prophecy is fulfilled.'"

Petra's quiet voice ceased, but a tumult of joy raged in Amaris's faithful heart.

Happy "Holy-days"

Lives are often brightened by those whose self-sacrifice changes holidays to "holy-days."

During one of the worst winter storms the Seattle, Washington area has ever known, scores of commuters decided driving conditions were simply too dangerous for them to be out. They opted to stay home instead of going in to work. Yet a short time later, dozens of those same men and women crawled in their RVs, pickup trucks, etc. and headed toward Seattle. Why? Radio and TV stations had frantically broadcast pleas for help. Hundreds of pounds of food needed to be transported from warehouses and donating companies to the charitable institutions ready to dispense it to the hungry in Seattle.

One man who drove nearly forty miles to participate in hauling food told a reporter, "It's my chance to do something for others." His response reflected the caring of many brave people who left the safety and comfort of their own homes so others might be fed.

During the same storm, the Gregorys sadly watched snow continue to fall and pile up. "We'll have to stay home this year," the woman said. "It's too dangerous for us to try and drive thirty miles each way." Her husband shared his wife's disappointment, but knew she was right. They wouldn't be able to spend the holiday with their daughter's family.

But the Gregorys reckoned without their son-in-law. A gladsome phone call a short time later announced, "Dig out your warmest clothes. I'm on my way! I'll bring you here."

Two round trips equaled 120 miles. But the glow of happiness in the older Gregorys' faces chased away the chill of winter for the caring son-in-law who drove those icy miles.

Neither Dr. Wu nor Bob Thomas were looking forward to Christmas this year. Dr. Wu's wife died a few months before. Bob's wife had recently left him. Both men were hurting but were survivors. They decided to lay aside their troubles and make the season happy for others. Each worked Christmas Eve and Christmas Day, freeing coworkers to be with their families.

An older lady, whose wrinkled face held peace, stood by her bright red Salvation Army kettle just inside the entrance to my favorite supermarket, one of many who sacrifice countless hours to collect money for those in need. It wasn't the first time I had seen her. No matter what time of day I shopped, starting before Thanksgiving, there she stood. Sometimes she rang her bell, being careful not to annoy any Grinch or Scrooge-like shoppers into complaining about her presence.

The little woman always laughed when I came, knowing I never had change going in, but whatever came back after I paid for my groceries would go into her kettle. On this final shopping trip before Christmas, I paused, smiled, and contributed as usual. Then I said, "You are so faithful. You should receive an award."

A radiant smile softened her face and a heavenly light shone in her faded, spectacled eyes. "I already have, knowing I've been able to help others," she quietly told me.

God bless the nameless volunteers whose reward comes from within, not without.

A guest on a talk show had an amazing story. Just after her mid-December third birthday, she heard a newscast about the many children in her area who would have no Christmas gifts. The little girl climbed into her mother's lap. "Mommy, I want to help. I want to give them all of my birthday presents."

"Are you sure you want to give all of them away?" the astonished mother asked.

Up and down, up and down, went the child's head. "Yes, Mommy. I really do."

Convinced, her mother agreed. Together they packed up the wealth of gifts and set out to take Christmas to those in need. Family and friends marveled at such selflessness.

The story doesn't end there. Each year, birthday gifts are very much appreciated, but givers know they will be passed on. The caring girl received more than four hundred presents on her sixteenth birthday, tributes to her one-person ministry. She kept none of them, for, at age three, she instinctively knew the truth: It really *is* more blessed to give than to receive.

From the Father, with Love

A certain rich man sat alone in his mansion on Christmas Eve. He stared at a brilliantly lit Christmas tree and the presents beneath it. His lips twisted cynically . He hadn't received a heart-felt or meaningful gift since his wife and only son died. Only tributes designed to win his favor and bring rewards to the givers.

A Bible verse the man had learned as a boy came to his mind: "Every good gift and every perfect gift is from above, and cometh down from the Father of lights . . ." (James 1:17). Oh how far he had strayed from the trusting boy who felt he had nothing, but actually possessed the most valuable thing in the world: Jesus, Savior and Friend.

An idea came, gently, then strong as a March wind. Why not search the Scriptures for those "good and perfect gifts" that the Father in heaven has in store for His children?

The man found his long-neglected Bible and began writing down snatches of verses, amazed at how many referred to God's special gifts. Among his favorites were:

"Peace I leave with you, my peace I give unto you. . . ."(John 14:27).

". . . I have loved thee with an everlasting love. . . ."(Jeremiah 31:3).

"For God so loved the world, that he gave his only begotten Son, that whosoever believeth in him should not perish, but have everlasting life" (John 3:16).

"Surely goodness and mercy shall follow me all the days of my life: and I will dwell in the house of the LORD for ever" (Psalm 23:6).

The clock struck twelve.The presents under the tree remained unopened, as the rich man knelt and thanked God for His matchless gifts of peace, love, salvation, and hope—then he fell asleep to the chime of church bells heralding another Christmas Day.

The Everlasting Hero: Memories from a POW

Charlie Montgomery was one of the last prisoners of war to be released. He came home with a lame left leg and a long scar that ran the length of his arm. But the look on his face when he stepped from the plane and into the waiting arms of his family just before Christmas wordlessly expressed his feelings. Home. Home and free. Free from the black nights, endless days, flies, the sounds and smells of war. Free to live, not just struggle to survive.

Even though the peace of Christmas helped soften Charlie's memories, he felt and dreaded the unspoken question hovering in the air: What was it like?

On Christmas night after the children had gone to bed and the flames in the fireplace dwindled to glowing embers, Charlie spoke, transporting his listeners to a world beyond civilization or comprehension. "I know you want to hear what happened. All the prison-camp stories you've heard a hundred times are true. The starvation, abuse, cold. I don't want to talk about them. Ever. Instead, I want to tell you something I'll never forget, the story of the bravest person I've ever known."

Charlie paused, stared into the fire, and began. "Ironic as it sounds, the eight of us who were captured at the same time spent a lot of time talking about heroes. Each of us groped for something or someone to believe in to keep from going mad. We listed everyone we ever looked up to. Our big Irishman Kelly said he didn't care if we thought it funny, Tom Sawyer was his hero. Anyone who could brave Aunt Polly's broom deserved hero worship!" His laugh relieved the building tension in the quiet room.

"Some of the rest of us held out for favorite sports personalities or military leaders. Juan Ortega, the youngest man in our group, remained silent. He was pleasant, but a loner. Not quite one of the guys."

"I'd seen him in action. He was practically a one-man army. That's why he was hurt the worst during our capture. He crawled directly in front of the enemy trying to save the rest of us. It didn't work. They found our hiding place. Anyway, Juan wasn't getting any better. He just lay on a pile of dirty straw, most of the time looking at a picture in the gold locket he kept in his shirt. None of us knew how he'd been able to smuggle it past the guards."

Charlie's voice trailed off. A long moment later, he continued. "One of the guys asked Juan if he had a hero. Juan nodded. 'Yes, but he's different than yours.'

"'How come?' Kelly wanted to know.

"'Your heroes are like the wind. Here, then gone. Me? My hero is everlasting.' He reached into his shirt and took out the locket.

"The rest of us sat up and stared at each other. Was Juan going to show us the picture in his locket, after all these months? Every man in our outfit had been curious, but something held us back from asking to see the picture. Not because Juan was sick. It was more the look on his face and the respect we had for him."

Charlie leaned back in his chair until shadows hid his expression. "Before Juan could open the locket, I smelled smoke. Fire! The whole place could go up in moments. We started pounding on the walls and yelling. The guards got the door unlocked. Kelly and I grabbed Juan and stumbled into the yard, coughing and choking from the thick, grey smoke swirling around us. There wasn't a decent place to lay him, so we sat in the mud and held him in our laps. He died that night."

Charlie's husky voice dropped to a whisper. He fumbled in his shirt pocket and brought out a tiny locket, bent and scarred. "We found this in the ruins. Juan must have dropped it when we picked him up. Everything else in the room was blackened: clothes, furniture, everything. The men crowded around. Would the picture inside be recognizable? Or smoke-stained and ruined? Who could be such a hero to a man like Juan Ortega?

"I pried the locket open with my thumb nail. Kelly repeated Juan's last words: 'Me? My hero is everlasting.'"

Charlie reverently held the locket out for all to see, then opened the battered case. His family crowded close. A collective gasp swept through the circle. For there in the dingy frame, untouched by the holocaust that had raged around it, shone the face of Juan's everlasting hero—an image of Jesus Christ.

The Gift of Wishing

Tinsel. Ribbons. Bright paper ripped and strewn everywhere. Three shining-eyed children surrounded by a wealth of Christmas treasures. Three shining-eyed children in the midst of Yuletide plenty. Yet I was not seeing them, but three children from more than forty years earlier. Children whose greatest Christmas treasure was the gift of wishing.

Every year it was the same. About the middle of November it came. A few days later, the other one followed. Stuffed in our rural route mailbox, the "Sears and Sawbuck" and "Monkey Wards" Christmas catalogs were the open door to every dream.

"I get the Christmas catalog!" How many times we squabbled over who got it first, once chores were done for the night, water pumped fresh, and wood piled high in the woodbox. Once a "wishbook" came into our possession, the rest of the world could go by. We'd never miss it.

Today's psychologists would surely throw their hands in the air in horror at the way our parents allowed us to dream over those wishbooks. They would admonish, "It's not healthy to teach children to long for things they can't have."

Who cared? We knew it was unlikely we'd get any of the things we picked out. Money was never plentiful and sometimes downright lacking, but we diligently made lists, wrote down page numbers, then tore them up and started over. Every minute with the wishbooks was like actually possessing the things we longed for. Besides, there was always a certain "someday" feeling, mixed with a "just maybe" or two.

At last the night came. Christmas Eve. The tree we gathered around had no lights for we had no electricity. Yet the golden glow from the kerosene lamps on the nearby buffet shining on silver icicles and decorations made from tin can tops was beautiful. So was the Christmas angel perched on the top branch.

One by one the gifts were given out. We had a rule that each gift must be opened and enjoyed by all before another was issued. There was no wanton ripping into packages. The curling ribbon that tied them was carefully untied and saved. Every piece of Christmas paper was handled gently so there would be some for us to iron out with "sad irons" heated on our stove and use in future years. Even now it hurts me to see lovely paper torn and crumpled into the recycle bin.

The smaller gifts came first: socks and mittens, pencils and color crayons, sticks and wheels (Tinker Toys). Warm sweaters, flannel pajamas, and cozy bathrobes defied a country that occasionally produced six feet of snow and sub-zero weather. A few Christmases were memorable because of a "big" present: the red wagon for my brother; a whole box of books for Dad; a doll nearly as big as I was when I was three or four.

Wishbooks remained important in later years, a boon for those living near small towns with limited shopping. "I get to get the mail" became our battle cry. How fun to bring in packages large and small from our mailbox out by the road! Sometimes back-ordered gifts didn't arrive on time. My resourceful parents cut out catalog pictures, then disguised them by wrapping them in several boxes and making them the prettiest packages under the tree.

What made those Christmases so happy? The gift of wishing, then rejoicing and appreciating whatever we received. I still see three tousled heads bent over wrinkled paper, stubby yellow pencils writing down the wonderful things we saw in the wishbooks. Most of what we longed for has come with time. We no longer have to count pennies and weigh one gift against another solely by cost.

When we gather around trees piled with packages, does the satisfaction of fulfillment ever really fill the space in hearts once held by the wonder of catalogs and pretend lists? Whose blessings are greater: those who give, those who receive, or those who once knew and treasured a lost art, the gift of wishing.

Command Performance

*L*ong ago in faraway England, troubadours traveled throughout the country, entertaining folks with poetry, song, dance, and drama. One troupe enjoyed several successful years before hard times crept over the land. Fall chilled into winter. Christmas drew nigh. Faced with finishing their season to smaller and smaller audiences, the players grew disheartened.

One particular night, they reached a snow-clad hamlet only to find the hall in which they were to perform cold and bleak. Even setting up their few stage settings failed to warm them. Worse, when they peeped from behind the dusty, moth-eaten curtain, they discovered only a meager handful of bundled-up persons had braved the bitter night to attend the performance.

"Give their money back and send them on their way," several of the troupe muttered to their leader. "There's no point in attempting to entertain so few on such a night."

The white-haired leader violently shook his head. "No! We cannot do that. The people have come expecting a performance." A wide smile spread across his face. "We must sing and dance and act and recite as never before! Few in number they may be, but these faithful folk deserve our best. Let us give them a Christmas reward for coming this night."

Inspired by his challenge, the troupe followed his command. Never in all the time they had worked together had they performed as they did that evening. They leaped higher, spoke with more feeling, and sang until the weathered rafters echoed their melodies.

The final curtain fell. The troupe clustered around their leader. "We are so glad you commanded us to give our best," they agreed. "Not only were the villagers entertained, our bodies and hearts were warmed by our giving."

The wise leader smiled. "It is ever so, my friends," he quietly told them.

The story does not end there. Even as the troupers rejoiced, a messenger well-muffled against the freezing night delivered a note to their leader, then turned and left the group staring after him.

"Who would tarry long enough to write and deliver a message to us on this winter eve?" a young lad asked.

The leader shook his white head. "I know not, but we shall find out." He opened the missive and read aloud:

Thanks for a beautiful performance.

It was signed: *Your King.*

This story has been passed down for many generations, reminding those who hear it of the importance of giving their best. The King of heaven and earth is always in the audience.

"And the King shall answer. . . Verily I say unto you, Inasmuch as ye have done it unto one of the least of these my brethren, ye have done it unto me."

—Matthew 25:40

A Gift of Comfort

One of my special childhood memories is when we drove the seemingly endless fifty miles from our small northwest Washington State logging town to shop in the nearest large city. Back then, Everett loomed as enormous to me as New York and Los Angeles do now.

In spite of my excitement and joy, I also felt fear. To get from the department-store-lined side of the main street to the five-and-dime stores on the other side, we had to cross Colby Avenue. It looked wider than the Grand Canyon to my country-accustomed eyes. Cars panted on all four sides, ready to spring when the lights changed.

My wise and far-seeing father never failed to quietly say, "Don't be afraid. Hang onto my hand tight and walk with me." The instant I slipped my cold, trembling fingers into his strong and tender clasp, I knew everything would be all right.

Dad is no longer here to reassure me. Yet each time I step into the mainstream of life's traffic, I can almost hear my All-wise Heavenly Father saying, "Don't be afraid. Hang onto my hand tight and walk with Me." My trembling stops. I know I will be all right.

PART 2
Frankincense

And the LORD said unto Moses, "Take unto thee sweet spices . . . with pure frankincense. . . .
And thou shalt make it a perfume . . . pure and holy."
—Exodus 30:34–35

Too Far to Christmas

"Miss McDonald," began six-year-old Jason as he tugged at Beth's shawl. "Are you going home for Christmas?"

Pain swept through Beth. Not trusting her voice, she shook her head and turned away from the watching eyes of her one-room schoolhouse students to stare out the window into a cold, gray sky. Enormous icicles clung to the frame. A few lazy flakes heralded the approach of another snowstorm. Why had she ever taken this job so far away from her beloved home?

Behind her, Jason sniffled. "Why ain'tcha going home, Miss McDonald?"

"Aren't," she automatically corrected before adding, "It's too far."

"Too far to Christmas?" Jason blurted out. His brother's, "Be quiet, it's a long way," cut short the accusing question.

"I wanna go home." Jason sniffled even louder.

So do I, Beth's hurting heart cried, but she only said, "Put your books away, everyone. It's early but I want you all home before more snow comes."

Ten minutes later the room sat empty and already growing cold as the dying fire protested, then scattered its coals before Beth's determined poker. She carefully shut the door of the pot-bellied stove, took a deep breath, and stepped outside. Freezing air caught her breath, and she pulled her heavy skirts closer.

No matter how hard she tried, Beth could not shut out Jason's words. *Too far to Christmas* rang in her ears all the way to her boarding house. They beat in her head when she stumbled to her room, thankful others were busy elsewhere. Taking time to change to dry clothes, she wrapped a heavy quilt around her shoulders and collapsed on the bed, a forlorn heap of seventeen-year-old misery.

Where was the noble sacrifice of leaving home to help out by teaching in the village across the great mountain? It had been bad enough those first homesick months, but the thought of going home for Christmas sustained her. She fumbled in her dress for the letter that had shattered her hopes.

We know you'll be disappointed, but we just don't have money for the train fare back after the holidays. Janice has been sick, and it isn't right to ask Doc to wait any longer for payment. God bless you, dear brave daughter. . . .

"Brave!" Beth cried. Visions of her hand-hewn log home that kept out the shrillest winter winds rose to haunt her. Laughter. Scottish parents reading night and morning from the Bible, the "Auld Book," they called it. Most of all, Christmas Eve. Nearly every inhabitant met in the one church for a special service that ministered to all beliefs. Beth's friends would be home. How could she bear not hearing the jingle of sleighbells as loads of laughing people clambered into wagon beds mounted on runners? Skimming through the snow behind strong horses. Oyster stew and pies at a farmhouse warm with light and welcome. Most important, celebrating the birth of her Lord with her loved ones.

Disconsolate, Beth rose and crossed to her window. The storm had passed. The mountain between her and home loomed white against a flaming sky suddenly free of clouds. Her pale, tear-streaked face reflected the color. It intensifed at a daring thought. If she could get across that mountain, someone in the small village at its foot would surely take her on home! Could she, dare she go on skis? Yes! Hadn't she hiked, camped, and skied the mountain since childhood? She and her brothers possessed wonderful health, a result of walking six miles each way to school, rain, shine, or snow. So what if it were the dead of winter? She wouldn't be alone. The God of her fathers, her own Savior-Friend would be with her.

Beth tackled the details the way she taught her eighth-graders to solve tough mathematics problems. She dared not take the train home and plan to ski back. Her parents would never consent, but would insist on her returning via rail, regardless of the financial hardship it caused. A reassuring glance out the window brought an even more exciting thought. With a full moon already creeping higher in the sky, if she started now, she'd reach the summit before the dreaded hour between moonset and sunrise.

Beth's lips curled into a smile. What would her hometown think when they discovered the girl affectionately nicknamed "Mouse" McDonald was the first person

to ski over the mountain at Christmastime! How fortunate that she had shipped her simple, handmade family gifts home some time ago.

Beth hastily assembled a light pack: food, extra socks, matches, a pocket knife, blankets—all the things she knew she would need in case of an emergency. Leaving a note for her landlady, she stepped into a wondrous world.

At the end of the first mile, Beth removed her outer wrap and tied the sleeves about her waist. Miles slid silently beneath her sure feet. Had there ever been a more perfect night? Evergreen trees cast gigantic shadows. Owls screeched, but Beth only laughed, too woods-wise to be alarmed. Only in church had she ever felt closer to God.

She reached the summit. "Right on schedule," she panted. The single great clump of evergreen trees she remembered stood waiting. Beth parted the branches and crept into a green cave. No snow there, just layers of fragrant, dry needles. Struggling back into her cloak and wrapping herself in her blankets, Beth slept as serenely as she did at home.

She awakened to scowling skies and a sense of urgency. She ate while she skied the last level expanse, then began her long descent. Not a wild creature stirred. Had they instinctively hidden from a coming storm? Should she turn back? "No," she decided. "It's as far back as going on." She zigzagged downhill, cutting off a mile. Her earlier delight changed to worry. Hardened as she was, could she survive if the pursuing storm overtook her?

"Stop it," she scolded, never slackening her pace. "You asked God to help. Now believe He will." Upheld by the thought, she took daring chances to cut off distance, unerringly pointing herself toward the village hidden in the soft folds of the blanketed hills. *What if no one will take you home after all?* a mocking little voice whispered. *It's Christmas Eve day and a two-hour horse-and-wagon trip from the village to your home. If you have to ski it, you'll still miss the Christmas Eve service.*

Beth refused to listen. A few hours later, she wondered if her nearly depleted stamina would hold out. The time came when only the sense of a guiding Presence kept her going. That afternoon, she stumbled into the yard of a farmhouse and offered the farmer a dollar to take her the rest of the way home.

He stared at the girl. "The good Lord Himself musta brought you this far, young lady. We'll see you get the rest of the way, and it won't cost you no dollar, either!"

With a little cry of gratitude, Beth threw her arms around the astonished man. Her long journey to Christmas was almost over. She would celebrate the birth of Christ, and the joy of being alive, at home.

The Angel's Story: A Fantasy

As Christmas approached, a great commotion arose in heaven. Someone, no one knew who, had started a rumor the people on earth no longer kept Christmas as they should. It spread from angel to angel, until all were talking about it.

"Not keep Christmas? Unbelievable!" exclaimed one.

"Not celebrate the birth of God's Son? Preposterous," cried another.

"Change Christmas to something else? Tragic," a third put in.

The Chief Angel called a meeting to discuss the situation on earth. "By now you have all heard the rumor," he stated in the gravest of tones. "There is enough evidence to believe it may be true. If so, we must decide what to do about it. Will some of you volunteer to go to earth and find out how things really are?"

At first, no one spoke. It wasn't comfortable leaving the beauty of heaven and living in the midst of sin. Although many on earth believed angels existed, others neither recognized nor wanted them. Yet as the Chief Angel said, something must be done. A band of twenty-five angels was selected to visit the earth.

The Chief Angel gave them simple instructions. "Make sure no one knows who you are. Find something on earth that represents how the world keeps Christmas and bring it back. Travel separately so you can cover the most possible ground. Peace be with you and with those on earth."

Many days later, the angels returned. That is, all except the youngest angel. Because of his tender age, he had been the last chosen. Now the angels worried about him, eager to give their reports, but knowing all twenty-five must be present. At last he came, clutching something in one closed hand.

The reports began. On a large marble table, the first angel laid a green branch decorated with silver ornaments. "It was hard for me to judge," he confessed. "Most of the homes I visited had lovely trees with many packages resting beneath. Many of them had an angel or star on top. I also saw numerous manger scenes, both indoors and out."

The second angel laid a pile of brightly wrapped packages on the table. "I felt the same. I saw people crowding and shoving to buy presents, but a spirit of joy prevailed. One woman said, 'If we had to stand in line like this any other time, everyone would be cross and miserable. At Christmas no one seems to mind.'"

The next angel displayed a nurse's cap and reported he had found many who gave up their own Christmas to help others. So it went. The items on the marble table represented those who no longer believed in Christmas because they thought it was too commercial; those who used the day to make extra money; those who spent hours soliciting for the needy. Some wanted no part of Christmas. Others stretched it from the first of December until the new year began.

The Chief Angel examined the objects on the marble table. "I also find it hard to determine how the world keeps Christmas. Some have nothing to do with the birth of the Christ child. Others are keeping it according to what He taught of love, concern, faith, and hope. If only we could be certain the true meaning of Christmas has not been lost to the glitter and excitement!"

"Excuse me, sir." The youngest angel slipped between two older heavenly beings. "I am sorry I returned late." He laid a small slip of paper on the table. "I too saw what the others have reported, but I longed to see more. I traveled from town to town, seeking I knew not what. I found and recognized it in a small home. It, too, had a tree and presents, a manger scene, a family sharing a bountiful meal. How welcome the Son of God would have felt!"

He stopped and wiped away a tear of joy. "At the end of the meal, the mother turned out all the lights and brought in a birthday cake bearing a single candle. The people joined hands and sang 'Happy Birthday'—to Jesus!"

The other angels gasped, but the youngest wasn't finished. He picked up the tiny piece of paper. "I slipped unseen into the smallest girl's room while she was saying her prayers. This is what she said:

> 'Dear God, Thank You for Christmas and my family. Thank You for sending Baby Jesus to be born in a manger, 'cause if He hadn't come, there wouldn't be any Christmas. I love You. Amen.'"

The Chief Angel's face broke into a smile. "Why, there must be hundreds and thousands, millions even, who love God and appreciate the gift of His Son! The world still knows how to keep Christmas!"

A great cry of rejoicing went up in heaven.

And far, far away, many children quietly slept in their beds, smiling in their sleep because they heard an angel song in their dreams.

The Belated Christmas Gift

All the packages had been given out and opened except two large, squishy bundles. When Dad reached for them, Mom said, "Deliver them both at once, please."

One in each arm, Dad deposited them before my two sisters-in-law. Their eyes opened wide. So did my brothers'. What on earth could Mom be giving the girls in those unwieldy packages? There was never enough money in our home for more than simple gifts, valuable in love rather than money.

The girls slipped the ribbons from their packages and threw back the paper. Through the mist in my eyes, I could see tears in theirs when they held up their beautiful gifts, gifts without price because of what they stood for.

That Christmas Eve was the climax to a story that started months earlier. Mom had retired from teaching after more than twenty-five years. She was close to seventy, having taken several years off to raise her family between teaching stints. When the first winter approached, Mom got down her old quilting frame to make replacements for the worn quilts we had used so long. She unearthed boxes and boxes of fabric pieces, representing dresses and shirts we had worn, memories connected with them. She set up her big frame in the dining room and began her task. Up and down. In and out. Tie and cut. Every stitch put a piece of herself into the quilts. For weeks and months she worked, blue eyes bright and keen. Then she spread the mound of quilts out for the family to admire. Each was lovely, all different.

She didn't tell us what she had already determined to do. Dad and I didn't know two tangible expressions of love and caring would be under the tree. No wonder I cried. Those quilts were gifts for a lifetime, created in unselfishness, given in love, constant reminders of a caring mother-in-law.

The story has a sequel. My ten-year-old step-nephew, who had been staying with us, fingered the beautiful quilts, then came to stand by Mom's knee. "Grandma, someday, will you make me a quilt?"

We all looked surprised. Who would dream a small boy would want such a thing? Yet the wistful brown eyes showed he was asking for more than a quilt. He wanted visible evidence of his step-grandma's love for him.

Grandma smiled. "I would love to make you a quilt," she told him.

I thought of the thousands of stitches, the hours of patience and persistense that lay ahead for Mom. Did my nephew understand? Yes, for he had seen what it took.

Early in January the snows fell, shutting us in from the outside world. Down came the quilt frame. Out came the fabric scraps. From them came a belated Christmas gift, one of my nephew's most treasured possessions.

Although Mom lived to be almost ninety-six, that quilt was the last she would create. Passing years left her hands tired, making it hard for her to hold the needle for the necessary painstaking work. Yet I often wonder how much more important than the belated Christmas gift is the gift of ideals and quiet example Mom wove into the lives of her many students, family, and friends?

They Were There

Seeing events through the eyes of those who actually witnessed the first Christmas often adds new understanding and fresh insight.

Mary, the Mother of Jesus

Great happiness dwelt in Mary's heart, happiness that started when she became espoused to Joseph, son of Jacob. Yet again and again she secretly wondered why the gentle man whose wife she would one day be had favored her above other maidens in Nazareth. "I am young in years, untried," she confessed in prayer. "Please, let me be worthy."

In the sixth month, an angel named Gabriel appeared to Mary, bringing a message that would change her life and life on earth forever. She had never seen an angel, yet she could not doubt the recognition in her soul. Why had the heavenly visitor come? And why should he say to one as humble and lowly as she, "Hail, thou that are highly favored, the Lord is with thee: blessed art thou among women."

Mary listened in troubled awe when Gabriel told her she would conceive, bear a son, and call His name Jesus. He would be great and called the Son of the Highest. Then she drew back and stared at her visitor. Her heart pounded with fear and doubt, "How shall this be, seeing I know not a man?"

The answer astounded her. She could scarcely grasp his full meaning when he said, "The Holy Ghost shall come upon thee, and the power of the Highest shall overshadow thee: therefore also that holy thing which shall be born of thee shall be called the Son of God."

Truth kindled in Mary's heart. She bowed her head and whispered, "Behold the handmaid of the Lord; be it unto me according to thy word."

Moments later, the angel departed, leaving Mary overcome with unspeakable joy and humility. Who was she to become the mother of God's own Son? Had it all been a dream? No indeed. She, Mary of Nazareth, had been chosen to carry the Son of God beneath her heart. She must find Joseph and share all that had happened.

Fear replaced her joy. What if Joseph did not believe her story? Would he cast her out when he discovered she was with child? She thought of what their village would think. Mary shuddered, knowing the punishment meted out to those who sinned. She shook her head. Surely God would not let her be stoned, when she was blameless of wrongdoing!

The angel's words, "Fear not, Mary: for thou hast found favor with God," quieted her fears. Trusting this promise, she rose and went to tell Joseph.

Joseph, the Forgotten Figure

Joseph, the carpenter, restlessly turned on his pallet, his thoughts blacker than the darkest midnight hour. His heart ached with unbearable pain. How could Mary, his espoused wife, have betrayed him? He groaned and buried his bearded chin in the crook of his elbow. Fresh misery flooded through him.

Mary's sweet face shimmered in his mind. He had loved her long, and rejoiced greatly when it was arranged for them to marry. Joseph pounded a fist into his other hand. There must be some mistake. No one so pure and innocent as she appeared could be anything but clean. Yet she herself had said, "Joseph, I am with child." Stunned by her confession and a heart that protested that such a monstrous thing could not be, he'd been unable to comprehend the strange story Mary told him concerning a supposed visit by an angel.

"What am I to do?" Joseph brokenly asked the low ceiling of his dwelling place. At last he reached a decision. "I cannot humiliate her or subject her to danger," he whispered. "Tomorrow I will arrange to put her away privately and not make a public example of her."

At last Joseph fell into a deep, exhausted sleep. Wild dreams subsided, replaced by another. In it, a shining angel stood beside him and spoke. "Joseph, thou son of David, fear not to take unto thee Mary thy wife: for that which is conceived in her is of the Holy Ghost." The angel went on, saying Mary would bring forth a son they should call Jesus, who would save His people from their sins. It would be done to fulfill the prophecy that a virgin would bear a Son whose name would be called Emmanuel, meaning, God with us.

Joseph awakened. His agony of the night before had fled. During those long hours he had been given the hope that would one day become the hope of the world. Rising, he turned his face toward the rising sun and stretched his arms to it's radiance like the angel in his dream. He must hurry to Mary and tell her what had happened. But first, the man God had chosen to act as earthly father to His only begotten Son fell to his knees and gave thanks.

The Donkey Who Carried a King

Little Donkey brayed loudly and started down the long, dusty road leading from Nazareth to Bethlehem. His master, Joseph, had no horse or camel. Just one little donkey who must carry Mary on their journey to a different country.

Joseph put his arm around Little Donkey's neck. He said, "It is a long way to Bethlehem, small friend. Your legs may grow weary before we get there. A great many people are on the roads going to pay their taxes, as commanded by Caesar Augustus. It will be not be easy plodding all those miles. Camels like to be first in line. Horses kick up dust that will make you sneeze. Hold your head high, Little Donkey, and step carefully. Mary is with child. She will deliver a King, come to save and rule the world."

Little Donkey's long ears twitched. Joseph laughed. "Ah, my friend. You do not know what a King is. It does not matter. Today and for many days to come you will carry a King."

Mary rode the plodding little donkey, glad to be spared from walking. Many times she patted the faithful beast's shaggy neck and whispered secrets into his long, listening ears.

If I had been the little donkey who carried Jesus, I would have been glad for the journey to end, but proud I had carried a King.

The Innkeeper at Bethlehem

They came and came and never stopped coming, hordes of persons seeking their own cities because Caesar Augustus had sent out a decree that all the world should be taxed. The inn at Bethlehem soon filled, and the innkeeper was forced to turn many away. Now he shook his head when another traveler inquired about lodging in his establishment. "I have no room. No room at all." He spread his hands in a gesture of helplessness before the tall, bearded man who had just said, "My wife, Mary, is great with child. The days of her accomplishment are here. She must lie down and rest, for soon she will deliver our son."

The innkeeper's gaze turned to the slumped figure atop a dusty little donkey. The beast's drooping ears showed they had traveled far. A pang went through the busy host. Such a young girl in the midst of the multitude! If only he had something for her. He hesitated then slowly said, "There is one place . . ."

He broke off. How could he offer lodging in a stable to the sweet-faced girl who tremulously smiled in spite of her weariness?

The bearded man cast an anxious glance at his wife. "Sir, we have come all the way from Nazareth in Galilee. We will be glad for anything you have."

"It-it's only a stable," the innkeeper stammered, wishing he had not moved his own pallet out under the stars so he could house yet another rich merchant.

The tall man's eyes twinkled. "We shall gladly tarry there, if your animals will not mind sharing their dwelling-place."

A look of relief crossed Mary's face, and she laughed at her husband's foolishness. Did her keen eyes notice how uncomfortable the innkeeper felt? Perhaps, for she smiled at him and said, "I am very tired, kind sir." One hand patted her swollen body. "A bed of hay shall serve me well this night, and prophecy shall be fulfilled."

"I know nothing about any prophecy," the innkeeper mumbled while he led his guests to the stable and opened the door. "There is clean hay and you will be sheltered from the night, should it be chill." He hesitated, wanting to linger but reluctant to intrude on their privacy once they stepped inside their temporary lodging place.

"Joseph and Mary of Nazareth thank you," the tall man quietly said.

There was nothing in Joseph's courteous manner to make the innkeeper feel he had been dismissed. Still, he turned and slowly walked back to his inn, wishing once more he had been able to better accommodate the young couple and soon-to-be-delivered babe.

If I had been the innkeeper, I would have felt sad my inn was filled, even though many coins came into my coffers that night. I would have treasured Mary's smile in my heart, and the look of gratitude on her and Joseph's faces, but ashamed I had nothing better than a poor stable to offer them.

A Shepherd Lad

Benjamin, a shepherd lad, lay on his back looking into the night sky. In all his young years of helping his father keep watch over the sheep, he had never seen the stars shine so brightly. One grew in such intensity that Benjamin rubbed his eyes to see if he were dreaming.

Fear and trembling seized him. "Look!" he shouted to his father and the neighboring shepherds who had come to make merry at day's end. "What is it?" He pointed a shaking finger at the radiant figure that appeared in the midst of light brighter than the noonday sun. Was it an angel, like the one that wrestled with Jacob so long ago? Surely not. Angels did not visit poor shepherds keeping watch in the fields.

The flock did not act alarmed, yet with one accord, Benjamin, his father, and the other frightened shepherds flung themselves on the ground, lying as if dead.

"Fear not," said the angel, for so the shining figure must be. "Behold, I bring you good tidings of great joy, which shall be to all people. For unto you is born this day in the city of David a Savior, which is Christ the Lord. And this shall be a sign unto you: Ye shall find the babe wrapped in swaddling clothes, lying in a manger."

A heartbeat later, a multitude of other heavenly beings joined the angel-messenger, praising God and saying, "Glory to God in the highest, and on earth peace, good will toward men."

A moment or hours later, Benjamin could not tell which, the visitors departed. One by one the shepherds stirred, then rose, staring into the sky which had become as other night skies. Benjamin's father was the first to speak. "Let's go to Bethlehem with all haste. We must see this thing which is come to pass, which the Lord hath made known unto us."

Benjamin's heart leaped for joy, and he ran to obey his father.

If I had been a shepherd lad that night in the fields, I would have been just like Benjamin and the others. I would have known great fear and great joy. I might have wondered why someone as important as the Promised One lay in a manger, instead of the finest dwelling place in Bethlehem. Most of all, I would have known that if I

lived to be older than the hills of Galilee, I would never forget the wondrous night the angels came while I helped keep watch over the sheep.

A Townsperson Who Didn't Know

*H*ow could such a shameful thing come to pass in Bethlehem?" the old woman sputtered. "Pah. It is all the innkeeper's fault! He must have lost what little wits he ever had, to send a girl ready to deliver a babe to a stable. Why didn't he bring her to me?" She glanced around her nearly-barren hut. "I may not have much, but at least it's clean." She rubbed the stiffened hands and knees that bore mute witness to the many scrubbings her home received and crossed to the open door, sending a black scowl toward the innkeeper's stable.

"Poor child, to bear the travail of birth without even another woman present." Her motherly heart overflowed at the thought. Now there were strange stories of shepherds rushing in from the nearby fields and coming to where the new baby lay in a manger. According to gossip, they claimed to have been visited by angels who said the Child was the long-awaited Promised One.

The old woman gazed unseeingly at the now-empty stable. If it were true, she and most of Bethlehem had slept or reveled through the most important event in history. Shame and guilt filled her. Why hadn't they known? Why hadn't the angels come earlier, so there would have been a fit cradle for the child?

If only she hadn't been so weary that fateful night. If only she had known what was transpiring in her own backyard, she would have hobbled to the stable and offered comfort, crippled as she might be.

Well, she hadn't known. Now she never would. It was unlikely those treated so poorly during their time of greatest need would return to Bethlehem. If they did, it would surely be long after she had gone to meet her ancestors. She drew her shawl close at the sudden chill that swept through her. Why hadn't she known? Why hadn't someone told her?

If I had been a townsperson in Bethlehem, I would have asked myself the same questions. Jesus, the Promised One, is still among us. Let us spread the good tidings of His coming so that none need ever cry out in despair, "Why didn't I know? Why didn't someone tell me?"

Wise Men from Afar

The journey had been long and hard, but soon it would end. An audience with King Herod would disclose the information the travelers, heavy with fatigue, needed to complete their quest. Hearts lightened. Urging their camels out of their slow plodding, the little band of men gazed at the star that had guided them long miles from their homeland in the east.

To their great joy, once Herod had been informed of the Wise Men's presence, he immediately summoned them to his presence. "You say you have come seeking a baby?"

"Yea. He that is born King of the Jews. We have seen His star in the east and have come to worship Him. Where can He be found?"

A strange shadow crossed Herod's face. He called together his chief priests and scribes, demanding to know what the prophets had written about where Christ should be born.

"In Bethlehem," said his advisors. "It is written that out of Bethlehem shall come a Governor who shall rule the people Israel."

Herod inquired from the Wise Men the exact time the star had first appeared, then bade the travelers to go to Bethlehem and search diligently for the child. "When you find him, bring me word that I may also come and worship," he commanded.

The Wise Men rejoiced greatly and followed the star until it stood over the place where the young child was. Inside the house, they fell down and worshiped Jesus. They presented precious gifts that had traveled so far in their saddle bags: gold, frankincense, myrrh. However, they failed to report back to Herod as he had ordered. God warned them in a dream not to do so. They took heed and departed into their own country by another way.

If I had been a Wise Man, I would have grown tired on the long journey. Yet I would have thanked my heavenly Father for every dusty mile that brought me closer to His Son.

The Baby Jesus

Baby Jesus lay in a manger, not a gold-and-jewel-encrusted cradle that was more fitting to His position as the newborn King. He had no welcome such as that reserved for royalty.

Did He care? No. Mary's low croon in His tiny ears told Him all was well. It mattered not that people outside the stable walls scoffed and said no one of any importance would ever be born in such a place.

All Baby Jesus cared about was the security of His mother's arms; the comfort of nursing at her breast while Joseph protectively stood nearby; the warmth of being wrapped in the soft cloths Mary had prepared many months before His coming.

Even at that early age, Jesus surely sensed and cherished the love that flowed from heart to heart: the love that changed the humble stable, in which the little family had taken refuge, into a friendly abiding place for the Son of God and His earthly parents.

PART 3
Myrrh

*And their father Israel said unto them, ". . . take of the best fruits in the land . . . a present,
a little balm, and a little honey, spices, and myrrh, nuts, and almonds."*

—Genesis 43:11

The Missing Angel

Christmas in the little town of Darrington when I was a child meant all the usual things: snow, carols, laughter, family, good things to eat, and Christmas programs. Plural. School and churches coordinated dates to avoid conflict, for half the town traditionally attended as many programs as possible.

In those days before God got expelled from public schools, our combination elementary-high school as well as the churches included the Nativity in their annual programs. Shepherds, angels, and Wise Men contentedly rubbed elbows with a beaming Santa Claus, his elves, snowmen, and snowflakes.

The year I was ten or eleven, the Methodist church had an all-girl angel choir. My heart raced when the white-robed figures with tinsel halos and lighted candles marched in singing. Would there ever be another such pageant? One where I could also be an angel?

Pageants came and went. Dozens of angels announced the birth of Christ. I was not one of them. Too tall, too scrawny, too plain to be chosen, I sadly watched the golden-haired ones proclaim, "Fear not . . ."

Years passed. Gray sprinkled my curly brown hair. On a particular Christmas after Mom and I moved to Auburn, I sat in a darkened church, reliving the Christmas story. Sadness that was all too familiar swept over me. I was too old to be an angel. Why couldn't I have been one of the pretty ones, one of those chosen? Didn't God think I was pretty or worthy enough?

Don't be stupid, I ordered myself. *It isn't God who casts the pageants*. The thought didn't help. Neither did feeling guilty for thinking that way.

The beautiful, blonde angel spoke. "Fear not . . ."

Bitterness slipped away. My niece Julie spoke her lines loud and clear, giving her best. Then it hit me. Had I not done the same? Had I not given my best in every part I played? In using the writing skills God gave me to create the pageant being enacted to the wonderment of those seeking to again relive the true story of Christmas?

The deep hurt I hadn't known I carried healed. Forever.

I've still never been an angel. I probably never will. Yet since that moment of realization more than twenty years ago, it hasn't mattered. Being my best does.

Last Train to Christmas

Ten-year-old Bobby Madden turned up his jacket collar and shivered in the bitter night. He widened his eyes, trying to see past the snow curtain that swallowed up the railroad tracks. "Please God, make the train come," he whispered.

In spite of his prayer, no bright stabbing eye shone through the darkness to herald the arrival of the long overdue train.

"We can't wait any longer. It's too cold for the baby," Mom said sadly.

"That's right." Dad sounded like he wanted to cry, along with six-year-old Cecelia. Bobby dug his fists in his eyes, too proud to let tears fall. If the train didn't come, they couldn't go to Grandma and Grandpa's for Christmas. Suddenly the tiny logging town where they lived felt like a prison.

Bobby swallowed hard. Why didn't God make the train come? It had been months since they'd seen Grandma, Grandpa, Aunt Connie, and Bobby's eight-year-old brother, Jack. Jack was spending the winter with Grandma so she could help him with his reading. Bobby thought of the old-timey farmhouse where they had been going for the holidays. Then he thought of the crowded little house he and his big family shared, the only one they could find when they moved to the tiny town where Dad drove a logging truck.

"If the train comes, we'll hear it and run back," his older sister whispered. Bobby nodded, but the snowman-sized lump in his throat shut off his voice.

Back home and warmed, the children sat with their noses pressed to the frosty window. Coats and suitcases lay nearby, ready if the train came. *It only goes through once a day, God. Please help us. It's the last train to Christmas*, Bobby prayed.

All night long they waited. Morning came, then noon. But no cheerful whistle disturbed the stormy day.

At the same time Bobby and his family waited for the train, Bobby's brother Jack slid into his Aunt Connie's car and buckled his safety belt. "Aren't you glad they let school out early?" he asked. "We can be at the train depot when the train from Lester comes." He bounced excitedly on the seat.

Aunt Connie frowned. "I'm glad we're out early, but I'm not crazy about the road conditions." She stared at the white world around them. "The first thirty miles will be bad." She put the car in gear and carefully started down the snowy road. "The last twenty miles will be okay. They never get as much snow there as we do."

"You're a good driver, and God will take care of us, won't He?"

Aunt Connie nodded, hands steady on the wheel. Yet in spite of her driving skill, it took over twice as long as usual to reach the distant train depot.

"They're probably already here." Jack unfastened his safety belt and squirmed out of the seat as soon as they parked. Yet when they got inside, only strangers sat in the waiting room. "Where are they?" He looked both ways. So did Aunt Connie. They checked the rest rooms but found no sign of their family.

"Maybe they went somewhere to eat," Jack said. "That's funny. Grandma told Dad she'd have dinner ready for all of us when we get home."

Aunt Connie asked the ticket seller, "How long has it been since the Lester train arrived?"

"Sorry, ma'am. It can't get through. Trouble on the tracks. It may take days to fix." He looked sympathetic and turned to another customer.

Jack felt awful. He loved staying with Grandma and Grandpa and Aunt Connie, but he missed his family. How could they have Christmas now that the last train couldn't come?

Aunt Connie finally got a call through to Lester. "Can you drive down the mountain? Oh, your car's not running?" She listened. "All right, we'll wait."

Jack's hopes died when she soberly turned to him after hanging up. "They'll call us back if they can get someone to bring them down the mountain on the back logging road. So far no one is willing to try it. The snow in Lester is much worse even than in our town."

Jack thought of the steep, winding road and many switchbacks. He thought of his disappointed family, away from all the others including aunts, uncles, and cousins.

"All we can do is pray." Aunt Connie hugged him. "Maybe God knows the road is too dangerous from the storm."

They waited in the station for hours. At last, the phone rang. Jack held his breath, waiting. This time Aunt Connie's eyes shone when she hung up. "Guess what! Their neighbor Hazel is leaving her own family and driving ours to the closest town at the foot of the mountain! We'll meet them there. Your dad said if it weren't for Christmas, even he wouldn't try it in this weather. Hazel knew they cried all night when they thought they couldn't come. She's a real Christian. She said she felt God wanted her to bring them and that He'd take care of them on the treacherous roads."

A few hours later, the two families met at the little town at the bottom of the mountain. Aunt Connie drove them safely home, where Grandma and Grandpa waited. After a good supper, the tired but happy people finally got to bed.

Bobby whispered to Jack, "Do you think God told Hazel to bring us?"

"Sure." Jack yawned. "He knew Christmas would be over before the tracks got fixed. I already thanked Him." He yawned again.

Bobby remembered the terrible drive down the snowy mountain. "I will, too. Dad called Hazel. She made it home before another snowstorm started. I bet she's really thanking Him."

"Yeah." Jack was too sleepy to talk.

Bobby closed his eyes. He thanked God for the kind lady who helped the Maddens when the last train to Christmas couldn't come. He thanked Him for taking care of them on the long, icy miles down the mountainside. Last of all, he thanked God for helping Hazel reach Lester safely so she could be with her own family for Jesus' birthday.

Gift for a Listening Heart

*B*efore "Grandma Pearl" (as everyone in a certain congregation lovingly called her) died at almost ninety-six, her hearing deteriorated. Active and mentally alert, she proofed and edited all her daughter's work. Yet it frustrated her to miss conversation and especially not to be able to hear well at church.

Still she set an example. Week after week she occupied the second row, right, front-center seat with her daughter next to her. The congregation marveled that she continued to come when she heard little or nothing of the sermons. They also thrilled to her testimonies of the "olden days," and how God had protected her many times. These included being trailed by a cougar on Thanksgiving Day, and losing most of her wedding gifts when a hand-operated ferry, without a safety bar, failed to keep an old touring car from shooting off into the river!

Week after week Grandma Pearl's daughter prayed her mother might catch enough of the sermon to be blessed. Yet she knew it seldom happened.

During one particular morning worship, however, a rapt expression filled the older woman's face. Her eyes sparkled, and when she got into the car after the meeting ended, she exclaimed, "What a wonderful service!"

Startled, her daughter asked, "Did you hear it?"

Grandma Pearl's blue eyes widened. "Very little, but I felt it." She laid a toil-worn hand over her heart. "God's Spirit touched me, and I knew how close we all were to Him this morning."

Then her daughter understood. God had blessed her mother's faithfulness by pouring His Spirit not into her failing ears but directly into her listening heart.

The Christmas Blizzard

Albert's icy fingers probed every corner of his coat pockets for matches. "Must have left them on the mantel after I lit the fire last night," he said. Peering into the growing storm, he blew on his bare hands, then stuck them back into the gloves he'd discarded in order to better search for matches. "Glad I wore this old mackinaw," he told the winter afternoon. During his years as a woodsman he had formed the habit of talking to himself, something that often served him well.

"I'm just a stubborn old man," he admitted. "Forgetful, too. I never go in the woods without matches. I was in such a hurry to get to Jane's, I didn't remember taking them out of my coat. Besides, it's only two miles between my place and Jane's. Who'd think the gray skies would become a blizzard when I was only halfway there? Or that daylight would disappear in the raging storm?"

At least the heavy tree growth overhead offered some protection from the increasing snowfall. If he only had matches there wouldn't be a problem. He didn't. There was no use trying to build a fire by rubbing two sticks together. Everything was so damp that would only work if one of the sticks was a match!

"Might as well face it. I'm here for the night," Albert admitted. "So what are my options? Can't take a chance on getting out in the storm and wandering around. I'd never make it either to Jane's or home." He speculatively eyed the trees around him, mostly hardwoods. Too bad their leaves had blown away shortly after Thanksgiving. Albert could have burrowed into them for warmth. One large evergreen had branches that started about seven feet up but were long enough to touch the ground. They formed a small enclosure completely free from snow, but it was so cold that if Albert sat down, he'd surely freeze.

"Can't leave," he muttered. "Don't dare stay. No chance of help before morning, either. Jane won't miss me until morning, unless she happens to call. Little chance of that, since we talked just before I got this big idea of surprising her. Some surprise."

Albert's eyes narrowed. His only chance lay in staying where he was, and it was risky. He didn't even have the knife he normally carried. With it, he could have cut limbs and boughs to make a warm bed. He'd noticed a nick in the blade this morning and laid it by the grindstone in his workshop to be sharpened. Just then a neighbor dropped by and by the time he left, Albert had decided to head for Jane's.

"Don't panic," he told himself. "Panic kills more persons than lack of matches or a knife. Think, man. What are you going to do to survive?"

Shortly after daylight the next morning, a half-frozen figure stumbled onto Jane's porch. "Grandpa?" the children cried. "Where have you been? We tried and tried to call you and the phone went out and we got stuck trying to get to your place and…"

Jane took over. "Don't try to talk. We need to get you thawed out, Dad. Children, no questions right now." She ran for coffee, hot soup, warm blankets. An hour later, some of Albert's sparkle returned, and he was able to tell them his story.

"I spent the night in the woods," Albert told them. "I had no knife, no matches. I had to keep warm. I didn't dare strike out away from the big tree. I knew I'd be completely lost."

"What did you do?" the oldest grandson demanded.

"I walked. All night long."

"But if you walked, how could you keep in sight of your landmark?" Jane cried.

Albert's eyes twinkled. "I did the only thing possible to survive. I walked around and around the big tree trunk under the branches! It kept me warm. When I got so tired I didn't think I could stay awake, I sang every song I could remember and walked some more." He yawned. "The storm let up when daylight came and I walked again, but this time I could see where to go, so I came here."

"That is so cool," his grandson said admiringly. "How did you know what to do?"

"I prayed a lot. Pretty soon I remembered a story I heard long ago, about a man in the same predicament I was." He yawned again. "I just did what he did." His eyes closed. Albert's Christmas blizzard was over. So was his ordeal.

Granny Hope and the Christmas Angel: A Fictional Tale

*A*ll Granny Hope wanted for Christmas was something she told herself couldn't happen. Time was running out. She would be ninety on Christmas Eve. Who knew what another year would bring? Yes, she was in tolerable good health, but nowhere near as spry as she'd been the year before. Why, some days it took so much energy to cook, wash, iron, redd up her house, feed her chickens and her big orange-and-white cat, Marmalade, that Granny fell asleep in her rocking chair during her favorite evening radio newscast.

Her greatest dream was slowly fading when an enterprising newspaper reporter decided to compile a story on the hopes and dreams of the ten oldest residents in her small city. Granny perked up like coffee in the old-fashioned percolator she refused to discard.

"It's a mighty fine thing they're doing," she told Marmalade, who never tired of listening to his owner's voice. Her work-worn hand stroked his soft fur. "The folks at the paper are going to try to make some of those folks' wishes come true." She laughed. "Don't rightly see how they can do anything for me, though." Her hand stilled and Marmalade purred deep in his throat, a gravelly sound that filled the small room with warmth and love.

When the reporter came, Granny apologetically repeated her confession. "You're wasting your time on me," she said. "What I want just plain isn't to be had."

"Oh?" Jerri Thornton raised an eyebrow. Was there a hidden story here?

Granny Hope leaned back in her rocker. A nostalgic smile crept over her face. "Where I grew up, we had a tradition. It was said that every year a shining Christmas angel appeared, but only to a few people throughout the world." Longing filled her eyes. "Those who see the angel must be worthy and pure in heart. I guess I've never been good enough."

Jerri's eyes stung. "I'm sure if anyone is good enough to see an angel, you are." She asked a few more questions, then drove back to her office at the *Tribune*. Hours later, she dashed off a final try at her story and left it on the chief editor's desk, still dissatisfied with her work.

"Thornton, get in here!" the editor roared a few minutes letter. "This needs broader coverage than we can give it." He waved her article at her. "I called a buddy at a TV station. You're going on the air with this tonight. Play up Granny Hope's story for all it's worth. It's got everything: pathos, humor, something for those who believe in angels. That's important. Angels are big business right now, and Christmas is almost here."

Jerri ignored his orders. Heart in her throat, she simply told the story of Granny Hope's desire to see the Christmas angel. She finished with, "If anyone out there knows how to conjure up an angel, please call this station." Jerri felt stupid, but took consolation from the fact Granny wouldn't see the story. She didn't own a TV.

Within hours, suggestions flooded the station. Wars and rumors of wars were temporarily forgotten by a country rooting for an almost ninety-year-old woman who wanted the impossible for Christmas. Now what?

The "what" became a party on the TV set for Granny's Christmas Eve birthday. She wasn't told the nation would be watching, just that the station wanted to honor her. Everything went well until a reporter from a rival station blurted out, "What about the Christmas angel, Mrs. Hope?" Jerri wanted to strangle him! Why had she ever consented to be part of this?

Granny shriveled and whispered, "I'm not good enough." Jerri wanted to bawl.

The announcer quickly said, "There are some folks here to wish you happy birthday and merry Christmas, Granny." Even Jerri hadn't known about this. She listened in awe while a retired congressman told how he lay wounded in a hospital during World War II, ready to give up. Granny's encouragement had pulled him through. Others told their stories of how Granny had touched their lives through the years. CEOs, lawyers, doctors making great strides in medicine and scientific research. Granny simply smiled.

The announcer asked, "After all this, knowing how much good you have done, do you still want to see the Christmas angel?"

Granny Hope looked ashamed but could not lie. She ducked her head and nodded.

The announcer gently turned her chair around. The camera operators zoomed in for a closeup. "Look, Granny Hope, there is the Christmas angel!"

All across America, families watched Granny catch the reflection of her own face in the gigantic mirror set up ahead of time. The cameras faithfully caught her expression of disappointment that changed to resignation. Then, as she caught sight of those whose lives she had touched, a radiant smile brightened Granny's face until she no longer looked old.

Hundreds of persons later called the station, insisting they had caught a vision of the Christmas angel in Granny's smile. Hundreds vowed they had seen something else, a white and shining image that flickered across the screen and vanished so quickly, they wondered if it had really been there at all. Still others pledged to be more like the woman whose peace and quiet joy proclaimed a life of faith and doing good to others.

Granny Hope never told anyone, not even Marmalade, whether she saw more that birthday Christmas Eve than her own image and the image of those around her. But the smile that lurked deep in her far-seeing eyes caused folks far and near to wonder for a long, long time.

The Very Best Christmas Present

Kevin and his little sister Candace leaned against Dad's knees. "We have a question."

Their father put down his newspaper. "It must be a mighty big question to make you so serious just a week before Christmas."

"It is," Kevin sighed. "We know God gave us Jesus, the very best Christmas present, but what can we give Him?"

"Give Him," Candace repeated, eyes anxious.

Kevin wasn't finished. "He doesn't need toys or clothes. He doesn't get to open packages, even though it's His birthday. It seems like He should get the very best present of all."

"Of all," Candace echoed.

Dad's eyes twinkled. "Did you ever stop to think how many presents Jesus received when He was born?"

"Sure. The Wise Men brought gold and frankincense and myrrh. We talked about it at church last week."

"Those are only a few of the things Baby Jesus received," Dad said. "Most of His gifts weren't wrapped. Legend says a little donkey carried Mary to Bethlehem. Perhaps that was Jesus' first present."

"Neat!" Kevin stared.

"You already know Jesus didn't have a crib, just a bed in the hay."

"'Cause the innkeeper didn't have room," Kevin put in.

"No room, no room," Candace chanted.

"We aren't sure whether there were cattle and sheep but if so, they shared their home and their hay with Baby Jesus," Dad told the children.

"Did Mary have a present for Jesus?" Kevin wanted to know.

"Oh, yes. The Bible tells us she wrapped him in swaddling clothes. She must have had them ready and brought them with her on the long journey."

"What did Joseph . . . oh, I know!" Kevin shouted. "He made a bed in the hay. If he'd been home, he would have made a real bed 'cause he was a carpenter."

"Can you think of anything else?" Dad asked.

"Well, the shepherds came to see Him. I always like it when people come to see us so I guess that's a present, too."

"Too," Candace chimed.

"The angels sang but that was to the shepherds," Kevin added.

"Something in this very room tells of another gift," Dad said mysteriously.

The children scanned the pleasant room. They looked at the decorations. They looked out the window at the soft snow on the windowsill. Last of all they looked at the top of the Christmas tree. "The star," Kevin called out. "So the Wise Men could find Jesus."

"See how many wonderful things He was given?" Dad smiled. "They all had one thing in common. Can you think what it was?"

Kevin remembered all they'd talked about. At last he exclaimed, "I know. Mary and Joseph and the little donkey and the shepherds and Wise Men all gave the best they had. Right?"

"Right," Dad agreed. "That's the very best Christmas present of all."

A little later that day Kevin showed Dad the card he and Candace had made for Jesus. It said, *Merry Christmas to Jesus. Our present to You is us, 'cause it's the best we have. Love from Kevin and Candace.*

"I know this will make Jesus happy," Dad told them.

"Happy," Candace repeated, and trotted off with Kevin to put Jesus' present under the tree.

Tinsel and Christmas Tape

Pastor Grey had advised countless persons dealing with friends in trouble, "It isn't as important what you say but that you be with people when they need you." He firmly believed it. A tender touch, a single flower, crying together all expressed caring better than words.

Now that belief came back to haunt him. The best friend he and his wife had ever known lay alone and dying in a military hospital hundreds of miles away. Getting a call through was difficult. The nurse had said in her message to the Greys, "Don't try to come. Elizabeth's so weak you could only see her for a few moments. What she wants is for you to send her a tape for Christmas."

The request sounded simple, yet Pastor Grey agonized over it. Christmas and death made a grotesque pair. "You have to do it," Mrs. Grey sadly said. "She took care of you after your parents split up. She even helped put you through college."

The pastor paced the room, feeling the walls closing in on him. "What shall I say?"

"I'm sure God will help you." She patted his shoulder and started from the room. She paused at the door. "You might try asking what you would want to hear most if you were in Elizabeth's place." She slipped out, closing the hall door behind her.

If I were Elizabeth. If I were Elizabeth. Pastor Grey's confused brain gradually quieted. He reached for pen and paper to jot down the thoughts pouring into his heart and soul. Once they were on paper, he could read and record them onto the tape.

An hour later he reread his list.

I wouldn't want anyone to preach. Elizabeth's faith was strong. She needed no preaching.

I would want to know I'd be missed. Surely Elizabeth knew that, but it would bear repeating. Dozens of persons would be deprived when Elizabeth died. Small gifts for a neighbor's birthday. Unexpected cards to struggling teens. Books and calls for shut-ins.

I would want to know my life had been important. He could remind her of the time they spent together, the nights he awakened with a fever and found her there, the hundreds of ways in which she'd supported him. He could and would tell her of the faith he struggled to find and finally won because of her example: a living representation of Christ.

Pastor Grey stopped reading and reached for a light switch. It brightened a stray piece of tinsel that slipped its moorings and floated onto the mantel. Beautiful and frothy, even though it was gilt not gold. Doubt gnawed at him. Were some of the things he planned to put on the tape more tinsel than real gold?

The pastor leaned back and prayed, "God, help me to say what she really needs to hear. If I were Elizabeth, what would be the final message needed to change a friendly message to a real Christmas gift?" Suddenly it came, the thing his message lacked.

I would want to know my friend believed with all his heart this was not the end. That he looked forward to being with me again someday.

Excitement poured through the pastor. This was the real meaning of Christmas. Not just the birth of the Christ-child but knowledge of the Resurrection. He switched on the tape recorder and went through the early items. Then he paused.

"Elizabeth," he brokenly said. "I will miss you terribly, but this is not the end. It's only the closing of one chapter in a life well lived for Him. I won't say goodbye, dear friend. Just, 'til we meet again."

He rewound the tape, shut off the recorder, and laid the tape on the mantel. It no longer looked incongruous next to the piece of tinsel lying beside it.

The Stranger's Visit

Bill Trevor* sheltered his lantern from a bitter wind gust and stamped from the barn to the white-carpeted back porch of his old farmhouse home in northwest Washington State. Snow had steadily attacked the earth until midafternoon, then thickened the sky to such gray gloom, the chickens thought night had come and went to roost early. A wicked wind rose. It tossed mufflers and bit through heavy coats and mittens.

"It's a good thing we got the cows milked and the animals fed and cared for early," Bill muttered. The wind caught his words and hurled them back against his teeth. The young man, still in his teens, shivered and fumbled for the doorknob. He had never seen a winter storm like this and he'd just as soon not see another. Ever. Woe to anyone far from home tonight! The heavy door swung open. Bill stepped into the warm kitchen and a blast of icy air followed. It fluttered the curtains and made the flames in the kerosene lamps flicker.

"Shut the door quick," his little sister Lucy ordered. "We have to keep baby Jim warm."

Bill's spirits dropped. He slammed the door, then shrugged out of his snow-laden coat and hung it on a hook, with a pan beneath to catch the drips. "I hoped he would be better."

"I don't know." Tears leaped to Lucy's brown eyes. "At least he's sleeping."

Bill's second sister, Alza, looked disconsolate. "We thought sure the medicine the doctor brought earlier today would break Jim's fever."

The doctor's charge while he measured medicine into a bottle earlier that day rang in Bill's ears. *Keep the child warm. Give him this. The fever should run its course.* The kindly physician had pulled his coat collar high and wearily trudged to his horse and buggy. Five long miles to Darrington lay ahead of him. If he didn't leave now, the rutted road would be impassable, and he had other patients to attend. Besides, he had done all he could for the feverish baby.

Jim slept most of the afternoon. The family rejoiced, although the storm became a full-scale blizzard and the deepening snow swirled into fantastic patterns. Mrs. Trevor and the girls prepared a good supper. Her husband, Lewis, blessed the food.

"We give Thee thanks, Father, for that which we are about to receive. Bless us and keep us, for Jesus' sake. Amen."

A hoarse cough interrupted the "Amen" that echoed around the table. Mrs. Trevor sprang to the handmade cradle in the corner and put her lips to Jim's forehead. "He's burning up!"

Bill leaped from his place at the table. Surely the medicine should have worked by now. "Shall I ride for the doctor?" His question brought heavy silence. On a night like this? Impossible! Yet even little Lucy knew her big brother would go if their parents agreed.

Mrs. Trevor shook her head. "You'd never get through. Besides, the doctor can't do anything else. I'll see if I can cool him by sponging him off." She gently uncovered the fretful child. "Don't open a door until I'm finished. Now eat your supper."

"Ma's a good nurse," Lewis quietly reminded his family. His comment reassured the family, and they silently finished the meal. The girls cleared the table and did the dishes. The fireplace roared, gobbling up great lengths of logs and heating the big room. Bill and his younger brother, Bob, sat on the wood floor and mended harness.

Hours passed, but no one made a move toward bed. The storm increased. Something thumped hard on the front door. Bill raised his head. "What's that?" The thump came again. He crossed the room and opened the door. A stranger stood on the wide front porch.

"Come in, man!" Bill motioned the snow-encrusted figure into the room and shut out the terrible night. "Warm yourself. I'll see to your horse."

The stranger smiled. "I have no horse. Do you have anything for me to eat?"

Bill snapped his open mouth shut. No one in his right mind would be out on a night like this, let alone afoot.

Mrs. Trevor called from Jim's side, "Don't keep the poor man standing in his wet coat, Lewis. Girls, give our visitor something to eat."

Lucy and Alza sprang to obey. They quickly filled a plate with the scanty remains of supper. Cornbread, still a little warm. Beans. Pickle relish. A glass of milk. "I'm sorry it isn't more," Lucy apologized. "It's all we have."

The stranger gazed at her tangled curls and sweet face. "This will be fine." He began eating. The family politely went on with other things, although Bill wanted to stare at the stranger who came out of a storm to their isolated farmhouse. Suddenly, Jim cried out.

"He's sick," Alza said. "But Ma's a good nurse."

"Don't worry," the stranger told her. "The baby will be fine." He went on eating. When he finished, he stood. "Thank you for the food. I'll be going now." Before anyone could speak, he slipped into his coat and went out the front door.

"Stop him," Lewis commanded. "He can stay with us tonight."

Bill ran to the door and flung it wide. "Come back," he shouted through chattering teeth. Only the dying wind replied. "We have room for you, Mister," Bill called again. When he received no answer, he came back inside. "Light a lantern for me while I put on my coat."

Moments later Bill stepped outside and shut the door behind him. Holding the lantern high, he peered down, then ahead. He gasped and jerked the door open. "Come here, Pa." His voice sounded strange, even to himself.

Lewis Trevor opened the door. The other children crowded behind him. Lantern light mingled with the light from the room and faithfully illuminated porch, steps, and front yard. The snow lay deep and heavy.

Not a single footprint broke the unblemished drifts.

The family stared, heedless of the freezing cold, until Lewis Trevor sent the girls inside. Bill shook his head in bewilderment. "The stranger came out this door. We all saw him. Where is he? Where did he go?"

No one had an answer. Lewis and his boys searched the porch, the steps, the yard. Only their footprints showed in the expanse of white that stretched from house to trees.

"Ma says come quick," Lucy hollered from the doorway. "Hurry!"

They fearfully rushed back inside. Was Jim worse? No, for Ma smiled at them across the room. "The fever is broken. Jim is sleeping peacefully."

"Praise the Lord!" Lewis exclaimed.

Bill's heart and the others' faces echoed the fervent thanks. Yet something teased at the young man's mind. "He said Jim would be fine. Who was he, Pa? Where did he go?"

Pa's blue eyes looked into those of his oldest son, so like his own. He reached for the well-used family Bible and opened it to Hebrews 13:2. "Be not forgetful to entertain strangers: for thereby some have entertained angels unawares," he read.

Lucy gasped. "Pa, was the stranger an angel?"

Bill's heart thumped. His mouth dried. Was it … could it be . . .?

His father closed the worn Bible and solemnly said. "I do not know. I do know no man can walk in the snow without leaving tracks."

These events took place more than eighty years ago. Witnesses' accounts of the stranger's visit have been passed down, blessing many generations. Bill was my father.

My Christmas
Wish for You

*M*ay love, peace, joy, and hope surround you as
you celebrate the greatest gift of all:
the coming of God's own Son.

— Colleen